LOTUS
of the Lake

On the Children of Poverty

GURPAVAN KAUR GILL

LOTUS OF THE LAKE
On the Children of Poverty

Copyright © 2009 Gurpavan Kaur Gill

All rights reserved. No part of this publication may be reproduced, stored in a retrieval system, or transmitted in any form or by any means—electronic, mechanical, photocopy, recording, or any other—except for brief quotations in printed reviews, without prior permission from the publisher.

Scripture quotations marked (TNIV) are taken from the Holy Bible, Today's New International Version®. TNIV®. Copyright© 2001, 2005 by Biblica, Inc.™ Used by permission of Zondervan. All rights reserved worldwide.

ISBN-10: 1-926676-27-0
ISBN-13: 978-1-926676-27-2

Printed by Word Alive Press
131 Cordite Road, Winnipeg, MB R3W 1S1
www.wordalivepress.ca

This book is dedicated to my mother, Surinder Gill, and my father, Amarjit Singh Gill, who raised us selflessly with the utmost integrity and love; to my brother, Deepak Singh Gill and my sister Raman Gill who, as my role models have always upheld justice, courage and excellence. To my grandfather who stood for the independence of India and advocated equality for people of all classes; To God, my strength, courage, Truth, and my source. To the underprivileged children, whose resilience has awakened my consciousness to the realities of our world. Without their vision, inspiration, encouragement and support, this book would not have been possible.

Endorsements

"*Lotus of the Lake* is a beautifully crafted and stunningly evocative journey that allows us a glimpse into the lives of children living at an Indian orphanage.... This book carries an important message of equality, peace, and hope for the attainment of a world without poverty. Ms. Gill's gift in telling this story provides the impetus for those of us who are privileged to ensure that all the world's children grow up with love, education, health care, and a hope for the future."

-Dr. Natalee Popadiuk
Professor and Co-Coordinator
Counselling Psychology Program
Simon Fraser University

"The flow of the poems is like the River Ganges flowing peacefully through the plains of Northern India."

-Professor Avtar Singh Saddhar

"I love [this] book! Lotus of the Lake is both a testimony and a hypnotic mantra. The poetry helps calm the mind and replenish the soul between deeply touching tales... visited upon the most vulnerable among us."

-Dr. Hrach Gregorian
President of the Institute of World Affairs
Washington, D.C.

TABLE OF CONTENTS

Acknowledgements	viii
Introduction	ix
The Purpose of This Book	x

CHAPTER 1: *The Valley of Need*

We	3
Moon Call	4
Dharti Mata	6
Venture	7

CHAPTER 2: *Silent Stories*

Children	11
Images	12
Children's Home	13
Bloom	16
Cage	17
Rajesh	19
Home	21
Pools of You	24
Souls Without Holes	25
Desert Sky	28
Muskaan	30
Iron Doors	31

CHAPTER 3: *Slum Life*

Slum Life	34
Slum Drum	38
Maruthi	41

Whirlpool	42
Cold Floor	43
Sivgami	45
Coffee Beans	50
Migrant Families	52
Migrant Seeds	53
Migrants	54
Souls Unknown	59
Raju: A Story of Hope	60
Strength	61
Shell	63

CHAPTER 4: *On Poverty*

Waste Bin	65
Window	66
Mindful Eyes	67
Sonnet #1	68
Sonnet #2	69
Roots of Woe	70
Ode to Poverty	71
Money Talks	74

CHAPTER 5: *The Need for Change*

Stop	78
End	81
Cloudy Steps	83
Changing Statistics	84
Earthly Robe	86

CHAPTER 6: *United We Stand*

Solidarity	88
On the Wings of Hope: Fly	89
Unity	90
One Clay	92
On Tolstoy	93

Table of Contents

Urgencies of Our World	94
Global Solutions	95
Art	97
Awake	98
Seed	99
Suraj	100
Face of Gold	102

CHAPTER 7: *Knowledge, Wisdom, and Understanding*

Education and Human Security	105
Enough for All	107
Celestial Sky	108
Hungry Planet	111
Global Web	112

ACKNOWLEDGEMENTS

I would like to thank my colleague and friend Davide Cottone, who helped bring this book to life. It was his inspiration and belief in the cause of child poverty which encouraged me to create this publication. Every step of the way he read my work, heard about my experiences in India and guided me to tell the tales of the silenced individuals I encountered. In one of his emails he wrote, "...most favoured, brilliant and perceptive writer of poems... Pavan... I knew you had it in you... that your poems would capture dreams." His words stay with me always and so does his guidance. I am forever grateful to him. I would also like to thank Susan Hawkins, President of PEI Eco-Net, for allowing me the opportunity to embark on this life-changing internship. Her leadership and passion for social reform is remarkable. Also, I would like to thank Bernadette, Maeve and Jagan Devaraj for sharing with me vital information about the Dalit classes. As well as imparting knowledge related to renewable energy, organic farming and other social structures within India-- not to mention wonderful South Indian cuisine! I would like to acknowledge and thank Vanessa Goodall who helped review and edit portions of the manuscript. I also greatly appreciate the efforts of Soni Joon, my friend and colleague, who accompanied me on the second visit to Bangalore helping to confirm assessments of the Children's Home and impoverished communities in Mumbai.

Introduction

In this work, the dichotomy between the affluent and the impoverished, not only within India but also across nations and the planet is acknowledged. The root of poverty, from which so many suffer, is pulled from the dirt of its existence, exposing the need for universal change at a very personal level—within the self. It is through individual initiatives that growth can occur and ignite global change for child welfare.

Although many of the poems in this work illustrate the universal essence and impact of poverty, they also relate the life events and stories of specific individuals. In addition, this work attempts to capture the depth, experience, spiritual wisdom and intellectual prowess exuded by people leading the most disconsolate lives. By telling their stories, we may begin to understand the profundity of their plight.

THE PURPOSE OF THIS BOOK

*I cannot do everything,
But still I can do something...
I will not refuse to do
The something I can do.*

-HELEN KELLER

This book is a tribute to the children of poverty, their resilience and their will to live in such difficult circumstances. Despite endless daily struggles, they are hard working and cheerful—beautifying the world around them. Carrying such a pure and magnificent light, they bloom as lotuses on the lake.

After speaking with various community offices, NGOs and administrators in parts of Canada, Hong Kong, Bangalore, Mumbai, Punjab and other parts of India, we have realised that the best way to help is through innovative solutions and strategies promoting global education transformation.

With proceeds from book sales and charity efforts, a Children's Home will be constructed for the very individuals depicted in this work as well as other persons from marginalized backgrounds. The home will follow the highest standards of education and child care we can imagine. Through global cooperation, it will provide underprivileged persons throughout India with the means to build their own realities in a safe and secure environment. As it stands, the home will serve as a model school in hopes to improve the conditions prevalent in such homes across the planet.

Full many a gem of purest ray serene
The dark unfathom'd caves ocean bear:
Full many a flower is born to blush unseen,
And waste its sweetness on the desert air.[1]

CHAPTER 1

THE VALLEY OF NEED

We

From a mould
Of infinite creativity
Chaotic synchronicity
We are found

Each with gifts our own
Awakening rhythm
Beautifying creation
Glorifying the world

Not one is without music
A tune unique
Full of mystique
To sweeten the taste of existence

Moon Call

Floating in the endless sea of stars
The celestial moon does call
For all to look beyond the bars
Of this confining world of walls
And behold light amidst the dark

As the sun summons night,
Dripping Truth upon the world
One subtle spark at a time
Sharp as the edge of a silver sword
This lucent sphere does shine

Stands as proof that Truth exists
Among the blinding lightless sky
If one seeks to search deep within
One may discover the light
Aglow in every living thing

THE VALLEY OF NEED

In November 2006, I participated in an internship funded by the Canadian International Development Agency (CIDA) in Bangalore, India. I worked as a public engagement officer for an international non-governmental organization (NGO) conducting grassroots work with people from migrant communities, shanty towns, children's homes and orphanages. Having felt a deep inclination to go to India for many years, I was delighted at this dynamic opportunity. It had been thirteen years since I last visited India. I was twelve on my previous journey there. Along with my family, I resided in the Punjab for a period of four months in my parents' village. The India I had known was a place where the air was calming and cheerful despite the traffic of city streets...where the fruit trees on the wheat filled farms stood adorning the green, pastoral landscape. Every morning a thick but soothing mist would gently wake us from our sleep and reveal the refreshing morning dew. Walking into the warmth of the mid-afternoon, the tall sugar cane sprouting on the fields of our family farm invited us into a world of silent bliss, offering cane as sweet as sugar to eat.

I knew my journey to discover Truth would begin in Bharat—the world of extremes.

Dharti Mata

So many colours
I have seen
Sprinkled on fields of evergreen
Crimson skies and moonlit eves
Starry seas filled with mysteries unseen

I have travelled along paths of red earth
Crossed pristine rivers in wooden rafts
Travelled on the backs of sandy camels
Seen bodies burned in holy piers
Along the Ganga where souls aspire

Amidst marble castles and streets of cobble stone
Surrounded by silk-like lakes, I have heard hills moan
At the break of dawn
Of a history far gone
Yet ever present in the Earth's bones

A past which transpires
But never expires
As a valley, it deepens
Living on as an everlasting imprint,
A wrinkle on the Earth's skin

November 26, 2006
Bangalore

Venture

From rocks of green frost
I have **come**
To a land where thoughts are lost
To **become**
One who wanders free of peril
And learn
To exist, solo, full of will
Renew,
From **one** who fears **to** one *who* braves
Every challenge
In life's sea of turbulent waves
And **soar**
Above the chaos of capricious days

March 5, 2007
Delhi

LOTUS OF THE LAKE

"There are two faces of Asia—one is shimmering, the other is shivering. Unless the problem is addressed, shivering Asia will totally eclipse the shimmering part."[2]

While travelling in India, I witnessed unfathomed beauty. The power of the natural landscape and the elements offered me a peace and a silence of mind I had never before experienced. I noted the unity among the land and its people. The lives of many locals are intricately connected with their environments—they depend on nature for sustenance, strength and spiritual growth.

As I looked beyond the pristine environment, however, I saw clouds of poverty and strife shadow the lush lands of South India. As I did on my previous journey to the country—but as I had grown and matured, I saw this world with a new perspective now. Even as a twelve year old, I stared into the wilderness of slum communities and wondered why so many existed. Now, I understood why they existed, knowing they didn't have to. When I looked into the dancing eyes of the famished multitudes, I was amazed to see how so much suffering and pain could be part of a world so fruitful and spiritual. The dichotomy between the rich and the poor bewildered me. Along with garlands of hope, tears of defeat engulf the country.

CHAPTER 2

SILENT STORIES

Lotus of the Lake

Of all the people I met along my journey in India, the boys and girls in the Indian Children's Home and the Dalit or oppressed classes, are the most resilient. They stand tall in the face of the fierce winds which blow everyday and which affect them before anyone else. These people, who are forced to sleep on the streets, in tiny huts, or on cold floors, are the strongest. Well seasoned by rough conditions, they can withstand any conflict in life. Yet, they remain caring and compassionate to the woes of the world around them. Trivial and petty issues are of no concern to them. Living in the moment, they are survivors. They are priceless gems, as sea pearls betwixt tarnished shells.

Children

There are children there
Behind iron bars
On cold floors with feet bear
In barren quarters

There are children there
Small and thin
Wide eyed and unaware
Still they sing

There are children there
Alone and abused
Abandoned by the rest
Unheard and used

There are children there
Who laugh and play
Amidst sullen snares
Sitting in unkind laps

There are children there
Full of worth
Innocent and brave
Beaming with light

There are children there
In dark rooms
Uncared for and unfed
Let their lives not be dark
Let them bloom forth, as the lotus of the lake

Images

Smiling faces
Holding hands
Crying eyes
Abandoned lands

Longing for home
Waiting to see
Maternal bones
Longing to be
Loved, not alone

Simple boys, solemn girls
Face pain yet endear
Leaving their worlds
Fathom no fear

Longing for home
Waiting to hear
Paternal tones
Longing to be
Held, not alone

As lotuses bud
Mired in mud
Shining with dreams
Yet blushing unseen

Longing for home
Waiting to feel
Warmth unshown
Longing to be
Kissed, not alone.

April 2007

SILENT STORIES

Children's Home

In Bangalore, the State Children's Home for boys and girls aged 0-22 is a multi-functional Institute which serves as a shelter, a boarding school, and an orphanage for infants and children. In the Home you will find children who have been abused or neglected, runaway, abandoned, orphaned or who are mentally or physically challenged. Both the boy's and girl's shelters have the capacity to house over one hundred children. The boarding school is meant for children native to the State who are orphaned, under State custody, or whose parents' enrol them in the school. If children in the shelter are not claimed or are not enrolled in the boarding school, they remain in the shelter well into adulthood. In its entirety, The Children's Home houses over five hundred children, many of whom attempt to escape. Unfortunately, the Children's Home is considerably understaffed and under funded. Thus, the teachers and caretakers are not physically or economically capable of maintaining the Home and the children at a healthy standard.

When I was on site, for instance, there was a tuberculosis outbreak among in the girl's home. Many of them were quarantined, however, the disease spread rapidly among the over fifty girls residing there—they were not vaccinated or appropriately treated. The girls who were infected suffered from severe weight loss and weakness. Many of them were quarantined in dark enclosed rooms within the complex for a number of months.

Further, a number of children passed away in the home due to negligence and lack of routine health checks. One child, for example, suffered from a dizzy spell and fainted in the boy's home. To revive him, the in-house nurse gave him sweetened juice, unaware that he had type II diabetes. He passed away a few hours later.

Often the children engage in unsafe upkeep of the Children's Home and are asked to perform dangerous chores by the staff. At one point, I witnessed a child burn his leg when a large pot of boiling water, that the house cook asked him and a peer to carry, spilled over and resulted in third degree burns on his right leg. The in-house nurse gave him a mild ointment and left the room as the child continued to scream in pain for several hours. Eventually, the ambulance came, he was given sedatives and his wounds were bandaged. However, he had lost most of the flesh on his right leg.

  The children, often neglected by caretakers and abused by peers in the Home, do not receive the attention and security they require under such fragile circumstances. Despite these adversities, the children manage to remain hopeful that they will return home one day. They laugh at the littlest things and they live in the moment. Instead of pitying themselves, they are thankful for what they have and they value their lives. From them we can learn how to live and love.

In barren fields
They search for hours
Seeking to reap
Truth, love and power

Bloom

In many parts of the country, one may witness advanced and soaring India as well as the suffering of underclasses in the shadows of new growth. Constantly searching for ways to unite the two—where every part of India flourishes, not just the wealthy few.

Cage

The Children's Home
A place unlike all others
Shelter for those alone
From life's tormenting weathers

Here, they are watered and fed
With plain rice, sambar and bread
Clothed in ripped rags oversized
A fit for the living dead

In death they are kept alive
To satisfy statistics
And sign on the dotted line
For corporate logistics

This place they call a home
Is more a Children's jail
Where kids come battered and torn
To a life they're doomed to fail

These kids exposed to horror
At an age young and tender
Should not be hurt and treated
As feared public offenders

They should be sweetly caressed
By love, generosity
And soothing, inspiring words
Which give them new hope and dreams

This lost, dropped, abandoned lot
Should be our first concern
To heal, to feed, to adopt,
To accept—to love as our own.

LOTUS OF THE LAKE

They are us, with much inner worth.
When pricked they bleed, when hurt they burn
As us, they feel, breathe, scream, love.
They laugh, cry, hear, hope, dream, yearn.

And they must be free
To live fruitful, love-filled lives
In which to grow, achieve
Their potential...and soar to new heights.

Rajesh

I met Rajesh during my first few months at the Children's Home. Instantly, he made an impression on me. Somehow, his light brown eyes told me about his entire life in one gleam. Without speaking to him, I knew the pain he had seen.

The other staff and children at the home called him a runaway. He had illegally climbed a train from the state of Pune and travelled all the way to Bangalore. Government authorities took him under custody immediately. I was there the day he arrived at the home. Somehow, he appeared fearful, worried, unsure, curious, aware, and hopeful at the same time. He wasn't sure if he was in a better place—saved from the abuse of his cruel family—or in further danger.

I learned a few weeks after his arrival that he had been orphaned a few years prior, when his parents passed away in a car crash. He was sent to live with his brother and his sister-in-law following their deaths. For years, they violently beat him and made him work for them, while keeping his wages. With nothing left to call a home, he decided to runaway to Bangalore at the young age of eleven to start a new life. He said he wanted to remain in Bangalore, learn the local dialect (Kannada) and start work. He showed bravery and resilience far beyond his age. As a jewel caught in a crevice of filth, he shined through it all.

Lotus of the Lake

Rajesh often spoke about his life in Assam when his parents were alive. He resided with them on the family farm in their large home. He would often run after the chickens in the courtyard as he collected their eggs. And sometimes, he avoided going to school to stay home with his parents.

Unfortunately, Rajesh has been sent back to Pune where he is staying in a Children's Home until further notice.

Home

For many months
I worked in town,
At a Boy's Home
Filled with forgotten souls.

There I met many young men
Who ranaway or were ripped from their homes
Left abandoned and unfed,
Facing the cold world alone.

Everyday new children
Would enter or be thrown
To their native town or to another pen.
I was left sewing the torn.

One sunny afternoon,
A small boy entered the home
Battered and bruised,
Abandoned and lost.

Tanned from the Southern sun
His eyes were searching
For some sign of love
A way out, of uncertainty

"Agar tum mil jao
Zamana chor de ge hum
Agar tum mil jao
Zamana chor de ge hum"

He would sing alone with hope
For the return of those
Whose eyes were now
Forever closed

LOTUS OF THE LAKE

He longed for his mother
His loving father
And is joyful home
On his family farm

But deep inside
It seemed he knew
His lot in life
Was in the hands of an unknown few

He called himself Rajesh;
He had a pleasant, unforgettable face.
Said to be eleven or twelve,
He looked much younger than this.

His eyes were a beautiful brown,
Lucid as pools of nectar
Sitting tranquil in lotus petals
Reflecting experiences of days past,

His smile was full and wide,
As the distant crescent moon
Illuminating the dark night;
A single light in a sea of misfortune.

His way was humble and meek.
Steadily he walked,
Seldom did he speak,
Observing with wide eyes the unhappy lot.

When he imparted a word or two,
His voice echoed through the walls as Angelus.
If nature's rose had a voice,
I believe it would sound like his.

Silent Stories

At times, when we worked busily in the home,
He would surprise us with a song.
I would stop in mid stroke
Listening intently, imbued with love.

I realise now why it was,
Of all the children I met on my journey
Rajesh stood out the most...
Indeed, he was the picture of peace

Though he had only the clothes on his back,
He never pitied himself nor looked for sympathy.
Instead, through his words, his song and his laugh,
Rajesh taught others to live in harmony.

Even today, I lose sleep thinking about his fate;
Hoping everyday that he will find his way

Home.

Pools of You

As pools of sweet silence touched by the sun's rays,
Your eyes gleam in endless radiance,
Lucid and calm they stand absorbing the air.

Waiting patiently in wordless wonder,
Stirred subtly with dreams and desires.
Dotted with recollections of yesterday,

They sing, melodically, of loss and demise.
Rippled with joy forgotten and missed,
Releasing to the bright sky, woes of days past.

As a new bride in eager stance,
They envision new scenes, pristine dreams
And kiss the present with vigorous wonder.

They behold colour on white washed walls,
Reflect light of every earthly hue;
In arid lands they find fruit of Truth.

Amidst the noise of the chaotic world,
They offer a blissful peace,
As the gentle stroke of the silent breeze.

In whichever world you reside, Rajesh,
A world of splendour or a world of hunger,
The light within your eyes—within you, will never die.

Souls Without Holes

They work and waste away each day
Breaking their tiny backs
Cooking, cleaning, sweeping in haste
Dirt of the ruling class

They bandage their bloody blisters
Wipe clean their blood and sweat
Conceal abyssal scars and losses,
Drying the glum tears they have wept

When visitors come to hear their stories
They carve smiles on their fearful faces,
Tell tales "full of sound and fury"
Laughing at their hopeless cases

Still, they cannot hide the misery we see
Living poor, with nothing
 Facing frowns when asking to be free
Seeking love in fists and frenzy

We know they haven't seen comfort or wealth
They know not what they lack
With pasts filled with grim days and grief
They care little to go back

Sprouting from such uncertainty
Born to disdain and strife
Often orphaned by death unseen
Frowned at by those alive

Running or chased into the home
They seek solace and holy grace
Yet find that which caused the bitter cold
Beholding not a friendly face

LOTUS OF THE LAKE

As we, they need a peaceful place
In which to grow and flourish untarnished
Shaded from the woes of bitter age
Well fed by life that is sweet and garnished

May 2007

Muskaan[4]

While working in the Children's Home for Girls, there was one girl in particular who always stood out—Muskaan. At thirteen, she was quick witted and humorous. Every time I visited the Home, she was full of resonating energy. Her laughter and her spirit lit up the entire room. Because she was fluent in Hindi, I could readily converse with her. We spoke openly about everything—our families, native places, goals, and dreams.

Enthusiastically, she told me about her home in a place called Ajmer, Rajasthan. There she was born and raised until the age of twelve. She lived in a small mud house with her father as her mother passed away when she was very young. Unable to cope with the loss, her father started drinking heavily. He would often beat Muskaan when he was intoxicated. It wasn't long before social workers discovered Muskaan's condition; they sent her fifteen hundred kilometres away from Ajmer to the Girl's Home in Bangalore.

One day Muskaan told me about her desire to do social work and help underprivileged individuals. I was bewildered. Here was a girl who had faced incalculable hardships, and in spite of her circumstances, she wished to help those in need.

Unfortunately, Muskaan will not be able to return to Rajasthan until an arrangement is made for an escort to accompany her on route. This can take anywhere from a few months to a few years. She has already been living in the Home for one year. Now she waits.

Desert Sky

I come from desert dunes and melting moons
Dripping light on sandy, starlit nights
Where the watchmen whistle throughout to warn,
Those who may lurk in the shadows to bite.

Not far from my home, a Mandir dwells,
A floating white cloud above the world.
Calling devotees from every corner
To enshrine in their minds its majestic mould.

Around my neck sits a locket gold;
Within it abides the marble wonder.
Roaming, thriving, soaring within my soul.
Reminding me thus of my dusty desert.

In the sand castled land of Rajasthan
My friends and I sang until the day screamed
For us to return home to our parents,
Have a small meal of bread and beans, then sleep.

When my mother passed away there stayed
Only my father and I in our humble home.
He drank his sorrows away and I prayed
He would find peace through his pain and grow.

Instead, he found release in alcohol.
He drowned himself in dizzying drinks,
Coercing him to whip me against the wall,
Taunting him to bruise my spirit.

So they ripped me, broke me, peeled me from my life
And threw me on a train as an orphan child.
To face a dark, deathly, dungeon of strife
Battling, challenging, questioning my own mind.

Silent Stories

Waiting for answers to escape this pain.
Until, again, I unite with him.
I live in hope and endure disdain
I trust my father misses his Muskaan.

Every night I see Ajmer in my dreams.
Carrying my friends and father on Mandir steps,
Calling me, asking me to live in peace.
Waking, a smile is perched upon my face.

Muskaan

As a sweet melody of strings
Your smile, Muskaan,
Stirs the air with joyful brilliance
Reaching those near and far.

Your laughter
Opens the door to a new day,
New possibilities,
Where there is no pain, no dismay.

Your utter presence
In any place
Embellishes all that you touch
With a spirited grace.

Darkness does not exist
In your world.
Though your past has been draped
With shadows unsound,

You look beyond the boulders
Of disdain and adversity.
With your dancing eyes,
Somehow, you discover ecstasy.

Iron Doors

Behind iron doors
Their faces form a mosaic
Of hope, desire, wonder
Of loss, demise, defeat

Behind iron doors
They speak of Truth and love
They speak, in spite of their woes,
Of better days to come

Behind iron doors
They hold hands, laugh and play
They laugh at the game of sorrow
They play in laps of despair

Behind iron doors
They learn to accept their lot
Discovering a rhythm their own
Meditating in silence on gain and loss

Behind iron doors
They never lose their voice
They sing in all weathers
They sing of joy despite their fate

Behind iron doors
They are an ocean of wisdom
Their thoughts and dreams exist unharmed
There they soar in utter freedom

Behind iron doors
They are free
To live, to ponder, to explore
Inner worlds of peace

Lotus of the Lake

Behind iron doors
They open all gates within
The gates to mind and soul
And imagine realms infinite

CHAPTER 3
SLUM LIFE

Slum Life

During the current economic boom in India, the growth of the Indian middle class and urban living is forcing low-income farmers off of their lands. Builders are willing to pay "melt-in-your-mouth" amounts for farmland bordering major cities. The result—payment melts in the mouths of the farmers and they are left with nothing. Unable to afford housing or find suitable work in cities, they are often forced to live with their families in shanty towns doing menial labour jobs such as selling coconuts, driving rickshaws or working as house servants. Lost in the noise of city life, many of them fall victim to alcoholism and lie helpless on city streets.

UN-Habitat uses the term "slum household" to describe a group of individuals living under the same roof in an urban area who lack one or more of the following:
durable housing,
sufficient living area,
secure tenure
access to clean water and sanitation.[5]

Maruthi

When I was working in India, I visited a variety of public and private schools with children from diverse backgrounds. I was paired up with a Kannada translator, Maruthi. She accompanied me on every school visit I made during my five month internship. The children loved her. What I spoke or taught the children in English, she repeated with playful vigour in Kannada.

Maruthi is eternally youthful, joyful, loving and friendly. There wasn't a day Maruthi entered our flat without a smile on her tender face. She was continuously flamboyant, exuding positive energy which never seemed to end.

I learned a few months after working with her, that Maruthi lived in a slum. I was utterly shocked. Maruthi? It couldn't be. She came to work seeming happier than anyone in the organization. She was always neat, tidy and well dressed. I felt as though I had been slapped across the face. I stood in disbelief and horror thinking about the implications of the situation. I then asked Maruthi where she lived. She told me the area and I knew it to be the largest concrete slum community in Bangalore.

One day I asked Maruthi if myself and a few other interns could visit her home. Appearing reluctant at first, she agreed. Reaching her humble abode, we saw that it was a tiny two room area. The first room consisted of a cot and a small television. Four ladies slept in the room. **Maruthi and her sister slept underneath the cot on the cement floor.** Behind the first room was a small kitchen area. It was smaller than the first.

Despite their meagre existence, Maruthi and her relatives treated us like royalty. Even her neighbours came to visit. They bought us sodas from the nearby shop. We stayed there for about an hour. When they dropped us off to the main road, the entire community accompanied us while we searched for a safe rickshaw. Maruthi called us continuously to insure we safely reached our flat. **On our rickshaw ride home, my mind was infested with** thoughts of Maruthi's life. I imagined waking up below that humble cot and heading to work each day. Why did she have to live this way? How could they escape this slum life?

Slum Drum

Huddled in a muddled corner
Under a rotting cot
Stiffly laying crippled on a bed of rock
Like a weary worm against the soiled wall

In a tiny room 4 x 6 feet
Seen to be furnished solely
With a single manja and TV
Shared by a five member family

Sleeping in such suffocation
The dark, airless, bitter night long
Breathing mouthfuls of destruction
Perspiring fire-like pellets of poison

Waking to a worried mother
A father lost on a coconut hunt
A sister blinded by toxic waters
A brother stained with grime and dirt

Walking into the kitchen corner
A room sized 4 x 5
Stacked with morsels of rice and sambar
Ingrained of course with mud and mire

Cooking a humble pot of rice
With a side of boiled beans
To warm the blood from a cold night
Soothing silly thoughts of sinking dreams

Of a family drowned in nothingness
Melting slowly in a steaming sea
Whirling, winding, sliding, circling
The way the waves decide to sway

Slum Life

Opening again the front door
In shear fear and unsung dismay
To a trying, testing, fruitless world
Thinking of ways to float through the day

Stepping, tripping, dragging to live
Through the slimy slum streets
Pierced by the vile stares of stony boys
Scarred, sprayed, ruined by tears

Engulfed in painful ambience
Breathing the still stale air
Heart beating to sullen slum drums
Hearing echoed taunts in this sunken lair

To see this slum life leading nowhere

Those whose lives are barren

sleep without walls on dirt

In the rains,

they sleep on muddied earth

Maruthi

As the lotus seed
Grows from muddy streams;
Stretching high to face our sunlit dome
To bloom in grace above a clouded floor,

Your delicate soul
In all its splendour stands tall,
Rising above the chaos
Of the penurious city slums.

Your face, as delicate
As the newly made wings
Of an emerging butterfly,
Illumines every gloomy day.

No one can fathom
The root of your existence
Lies in a plain so barren,
Earth's naked burden.

The serene beauty
You exude, Maruthi,
Born to unforgiving poverty
Will endure eternally.

Whirlpool

Born, bound, bought in slums
Steadily singing, surrounded by dirt
Swarming fearfully, swimming in filth
Waking, walking, waning to death

Thinking, blinking, sinking in disbelief
Not believing this is all that'll be
In life, only strife, only misery
No escape from this soiled, empty dream

Endlessly searching deep within
For a spark, a glimmer, a beam to win
A golden ticket, a tinker bell, a God of love
To sweep away the dustiness of birth

All along falling deeper and deeper
As if engulfed in a well of tar
Submerged in its swallowing arms
Unable to break from its grasp

Beholding not a branch of hope
To grab, to clasp, to clench, to hold
In this whirlpool of disaster
From which not a single soul escapes

Is this the life any of us would want?
To exist overshadowed, in the shadows
As a shadow of a blind society filled with those
Who choose to ignore our drowning drones

Tell me, shake me, whack me, wake me
If I am wrong to think these souls
Who lurk in the back alleys of human woe
Deserve freedom from such misfortune

Cold Floor

Awaking early morning
On a cold floor
Ready to face life's rampant sea
Walking bravely to shore

Diving into the Deep
Submerged in cold water
Tasting the salty day
Welcoming in the World

Swimming in haste
To the cold hand of wealth
Knowing to be late
Would mean to swim in filth

Arriving at the door of the opposite shore
Feeling cold stairs beneath
Smiling from the core
Shaking the hands that feed

Warming the large room
Feeling the cold walls
Assisting all souls to bloom
Answering their every call

Listening to shallow complaints
Sitting on a cold chair
Not wanting them to suffer
Showing them love and care

Enduring belittlement and disrespect
From the cold city
That sneers at the impoverished
Stepping on their dignity

LOTUS OF THE LAKE

Heading back to shore
Sliding into the cold tide
Leaving far behind images of wealth
Releasing thoughts of this paradox

Swimming rhythmically to reach home
Allowing the cold Brine to wash away inner pride
Enjoying the feeling of letting go
Meeting like-minded souls of every kind

Reaching the destitute shore of birth
Exhaling now and feeling warmth
Of those without worldly wealth
Seeing light in the midst of darkness

Working again to make ends meet
Easing the woes and worries of elders
Insuring there is enough for all to eat
Teasing the innocent, unknowing children

Preparing for a humble sleep
Laying a straw mat on the cold floor
Bidding adieu the enchanting night
Praying for love, peace and harmony on all shores

Sivgami

Upon my arrival in India, Sivgami smiled at me warmly and made me feel at home. While inhabiting a room the size of a Japanese Tatami mat, she worked as the house keeper, cleaning and maintaining the four story flat we resided in. Still, she was never too busy or tired to care. When we became friends, we would share stories and communicate about our lives despite the fact that we did not share a common language. She spoke Tamilian and Kannada, both languages foreign to me. In our expressive conversations, she taught me words in her language like, "superla" (very beautiful). And I taught her phrases like, "good morning" and "how are you?"

Throughout the five month internship, Sivgami told me about her life in short snippets, which I slowly placed together as the pieces of mosaic—colourful yet fragmented. Married at a very young age, Sivgami grew up in the state of Tamil Nadu. Her husband was an alcoholic who didn't work or support the family in any manner; instead, he beat her and cheated on her in front of her and their children.

Left with few options and employment opportunities in Tamil Nadu, she was forced to leave her children with her mother and find work in Bangalore. As she was the sole provider for her children. Sivgami visited her family only a few times a year—if she could afford it. In over five months, she traveled to Tamil Nadu only once, to attend the marriage of her eldest daughter (who was twelve years old). **When I first arrived in Bangalore, I thought Sivgami was like us, but she was not. She was born to a very difficult reality.**

I recall an incident in Bangalore when a fellow intern and I were on our way home from kickboxing lessons in town. We took a rickshaw to Rajarajeshwari Nagar (a suburb of Bangalore) at about 10pm (a very unsafe hour for females, unaccompanied by males, to travel within the city). Unfortunately, we had no choice. During the rickshaw ride, the driver doubled his rate. We were very disappointed and decided only to pay him the original amount. When he dropped us off, I put the original amount in his hand and we ran up to our flat and locked the door. He followed us up in a rage and banged on the door.

The other interns in the flat were afraid and didn't move. Within one or two minutes Super woman Sivgami raced off her straw mat and out of her closet-like room, to defend us. She yelled at the large man and told him to "get the heck out of the flat...now!" He banged a few more times, ranted a little and then walked away. She then came to check if we were okay and went quietly back to sleep on the straw mat in her small room. I know we could have given him the difference he unfairly demanded—but it was a matter of principle and he tried to cheat us. Sivgami helped us uphold our integrity with her bravery. And this was not the first time Sivgami has rescued interns. A few years prior, a drunken rickshaw driver drove an intern home and when he dropped her off, he followed her into the flat. Sivgami heard the commotion and ran out. She told the intern to go inside and physically held the driver and drove him out of the flat.

Despite her brave and heroic character, surpassing the average individual, Sivgami is considered a Dalit in India. She has very few rights and securities as a citizen. As proof of this, Sivgami was fired near the end of my stay because there were complaints about her work abilities. As she was not part of a union or on a formal contract, she was given minimal warning.

Although Sivgami rarely allowed negative emotions to show on her face, when I sketched her portrait I saw deep into her visage. The fine lines around her eyes spoke of broken bonds. Her focused gaze searched for her children. Her wrinkled forehead revealed motherly worry and uncertainty about the future of her family. These thoughts she almost never revealed. She buried them deep within her sprit, to be found when searched for.

Sivgami

Your cheerful face
Stays with me
Until this day

It sits upon my window sill
Decorating
The room in which I dwell

Perhaps you recall that afternoon
When I sketched your face
My pencil played your tune

We sat on cubed rocks
Outside the flat
As you posed

I will never forget
How happy you were
When you saw the result

You showed all your friends
With hearty laughter
You hugged me and kissed my head

I hope your face
Still looks as cheerful
As it did that sunny day

While in India, I visited a friend's coffee plantation. There, I saw the most lush and beautiful coffee trees embedded in wild grassland, forest and still lakes. The coffee beans are incredibly pure and tasteful. Unfortunately for the Dalit workers on the plantation, the coffee is packed and transported to the local markets in hundred pound bags—usually in the heat of the afternoon. Following a tour of the plantation, my friend's mother served us fresh coffee as we sat on the steps of the estate. Although it was the best coffee I had ever tasted, it left a bitter film in my mouth. **I could not forget the images of those delicate frames carrying such heavy loads.** They too deserved to enjoy life. **Yet they were working ceaselessly under the piercing sun, as we sat enjoying our coffee.** For them I have respect.

Coffee Beans

For them I have respect
Who live simply without complaint
They have found true success
Who work long days in endless pain

Those who rise with the sun
Each day wake from a simple sleep
Sustained on hardened crumbs
Ungarnished, unsweet, tasteless "treats"

They are one with the land
Connected with the dirt they work
They have simple demands
Using shovels not swords

They have neither ego nor greed
All they ask is to have enough
They want not luxury
Only warmth, shelter and love

For them I have respect
Who live simply yet don't complain
They live not in excess
And cannot show disdain

They are not big or tall
Yet they're stronger than those who are
They lift a heavy weight
Moving mounds of brick, stone and tar

My eyes have seen them with
Hundred pound bags of coffee beans
Thus carried on their hips
All day without breaking a beat

Slum Life

Sweating and breathing hard
I have witnessed their bravery
With boulders on their heads
Walking miles to the city

For them I have respect
Who live simply yet don't complain
Those who the world rejects
I applaud their will everyday

June 13, 2007

Migrant Families

Although there are many migrant communities dispersed throughout India, the families I speak about in "Migrant Seeds" were based in Bangalore. The migrants work on construction sites in many growing communities and help to build apartments, homes or government structures in the area. This may take anywhere from several months to many years. **Often in unsafe working conditions, they work long, arduous hours. They have only enough to support the bare necessities of their families as they receive very little pay.**

Although children under fourteen are not legally allowed to work in Karnataka State, they often assist their parents with shovelling, transporting materials and cleaning. In addition, underage children are often left to handle the household while their parents are away working. This includes cooking, cleaning, collecting water from the local water source, and raising their younger siblings. When the children turn fourteen they join their parents on the construction sites. Although there were many teenagers in the migrant community, we had very few kids over the age of thirteen in our class.

Migrant Seeds

I met a few migrant seeds
Sown in various migrant fields
Buried, reaped then plucked
And sent away on tattered trucks

These seeds don't live as you or I
No home is there own to throne
They choose **not** the path of their lives
They catch what they are thrown

In eager retrieve
Floating from land to land
Sinking in fields bereaved
Sprouting to shouting demands

Following harsh commands
Of the **leaders of** the land
Singing the melodies of **their dreams**
Rhyming to the rhythm of their needs

June 20, 2007

Migrants

A community of migrant workers
Lived across our hostel door
Families of 4, 5, 6 or 7
Camped in blue tarped tents

We happily asked the children there
To join us for school and snacks to share
And a few games of play
As they'd never been taught this way

Without fail they would join us everyday
Arriving with their friends and families, never late
In fact some days they would wait
For the class to start at our gate

The migrant kids entered as a whirlwind
Shaking the room and all within it
They would smile round as rainbows
Colouring the room with their eyes aglow

Their presence was a lightening storm
They excited and brightened the flat with splendour
Their laughter blew in howling breezes
Their witty thoughts made us laugh and cheer

Cluttering, clattering, chattering, they arrived
Wandering round the room in full swing
Before finally spreading the carpet
To sit and learn the lesson

In the class they would fly
As kites in a clear blue sky
They would sway as sails
As rippling waves, as floating flames

Slum Life

With us, they would sing
Like young birds learning
To chirp in twine
Battling with their lungs in chime

After a lesson on the alphabet
We played silly games they loved
Like Duck Duck Goose
We danced to silly songs and let loose

Some spent the entire class
With their siblings clasped
Close to their beating hearts
As aprons wrapped around their waists

These children raised their siblings
Caring for them without release
Protecting them as mothers
Sheltering them as fathers

What they had they shared
With the younger bred
What they learned they taught
To the littler lot

Asking the kids to wash their hands
Was an arduous task
They would sprint to the water tap
Slap on a speck of soap and run to have their snack

When the smell of food was near
They would run about and cheer
Eagerly awaiting an egg or bread
To stuff into their hungry mouths, unfed

LOTUS OF THE LAKE

As the class came to an end
They would hide, run and pretend
Do anything they could do
To stay and play another minute or two

It seems they found our flat
More inviting than the tattered tents
In which they lived as gypsies
Blowing with the breeze every season

One day I asked the wee migrants
If they would take me into their camp
To see exactly how they lived
Why when they came they wouldn't leave

They took me by the hand
And ran with me to their blue land
It looked as a plastic sea of waves
It smelled as stale as rotted bread

The tents were nothing more than what they seemed
Their "homes" were filled with dirt and need
They were as barren as hollow trees
Carrying only piles of rags, rice and a few seeds

At the dirt floor, I stared stunned
Stone cold, gunned
Shot in my heart, fiercely pierced
By the cold, cruel hand of poverty

There I died I died I died
I showed no emotion but within I cried
I shouted I yelled I screamed
To the world asking why? How can this be?

Slum Life

These parents, kids, babies
Lived with nothing, immersed in filth, in nothing
We across the way.... lived in a home
With a bed, a room, a flat, a bath a stove our own

How is this, what it is?
Why the difference?
Why this injustice?
Our **indifference.**

I understood that day
Why the migrant kids would stay
And wait for us for hours everyday
In front of our flat this way

Never did I ask them again
To hurry home at the end of the school day

                                                                     June 23, 2007

Look beyond their flesh

Peer within their eyes

Discover what it is they search

What dreams within they hide

Seek and you will see

The essence of who they are

The Truth of this worldly dream

The light in every shattered star

Souls Unknown

Souls unknown;
Those we all claim to know.

We know their flesh,
Their barren bones

We know their hunger;
Their thirst unquenched.

Bearing naked needs,
Their desperate pleas.

This lot struck hard
By unlucky stars

Dealt a bad hand
A fruitless land

We know their ills
Their plates unfilled

We know the deathly mess
Of their earthly flesh

We know their tears
Rolling as streams

Down the swollen valleys
Of their hollow cheeks.

Them, their souls, alas,
Their inner Truth,

Desires, dreams uncast
Inner worth, to the world

Remain unknown

Raju: A Story of Hope

At the NGO office where I lived and worked, two small cooperatives were run with the help of local Dalits—hand made paper cards and stitched, cotton hand bags. A youth named Raju conceptualized the idea. Coming from a Dalit family, Raju decided he wanted to have a better life. He was one of the first students to attend a children's school at the Office. Doing well in the classes, Raju strove to complete his high school education. Upon completion, he realised his innate ability in the Arts. Approaching the coordinators at the NGO, he asked if he could work for them making cards using print screens. Noting the brilliance of the idea, they agreed to help him and applied for project funding.

The project has turned out to be a huge success. Today, Raju still works for the NGO designing prints, greeting cards, wedding cards, and other hand made paper products to be sold in various markets throughout the UK and India. He uses his wages to pay for his college tuition. He plans to complete his B.A. in Economics.

As Raju, all Dalits and other underprivileged persons have the right to achieve their purpose. If we help them unlock their inner worth and beauty, they will help enrich the world in which we live. **They too are humans who should be seen, not as servants to society, but as creative, intuitive beings with infinite potential.**

Strength

They have more strength I see
They have the strength of liberty
They who walk roads low and cold
Shadows of our growing world

They walk with integrity
Breaking walls, accepting all
They hold out their hands for everyone
They do not judge at all

As young children with sweet thoughts
Birds with weightless wings
They fly with grace from branch to branch
On the tree of life they sing

They have more strength I see
They have the strength of liberty
Living abundantly
Without health, wealth, prosperity

Those we do not see
Upon whose limbs we walk
They see more Truth than we
Stand closer to infinity

They are not envious
Of pleasures others have
They look within themselves
Find strength to carry on

LOTUS OF THE LAKE

They have more strength I see
Now I see they have the strength of liberty
They work with what they have
Don't dwell in misery

They have more strength I see
They have the strength of liberty

Shell

Judging your outer, weathered shell,
Your slim, slight outer case,
Your slender, child-like frame,
Alight with your sly, musing smile,

One cannot clearly conceive
What lies beneath your tender
Impoverished bodice.
Our flesh muddies our inner seas.

Only peering through the windows
Of your telling, brown eyes
Do I discover your light,
Revealing the essence of your soul.

Exposing your inner passions
For art, writing and love.
Your wish to soar above
The shattered life of the slums.

Your fierce, fire-like drive to survive;
Withstanding unbounded
Wind blown through your shanty town.
Building realization

Of inherent, gifted talents
And aesthetic mind.
Which enrich your inner being,
As water pearls enrich the brine.

I have seen the will-full way you
Work from your soul to your pen,
When making a print or sketch;
Each one is an imprint of your truth.

SECTION 4

ON POVERTY

Waste Bin

Today I saw him swimming through
The rubbish of our wasteful ways
Sorting, sifting, unable to
Find a mere morsel to sustain

His bent up body which had been
Robbed of vigour, health and love
Stripped of colour and of beauty
Looking as though a mangled log

I pained, waned, feigned at his site
Trying not to scream out loud
Seeing my own in such sore plight
Made me want to wake up the world

Despite the strife of this poor man
I know, I sense, his soul still stands
As tall and broad as soldiers can
As bright as any beaming star

July 2007
Vancouver

Window

Standing behind a tall, shielding window,
Warm, secure, untouched
By that which infects the world beyond,
I watch them cold, broken, defenceless

So far away from comfort
I cannot reach, only see
And repent that which unfolds
Only ask, how can this be?

In my cushioned world
Filled with all pleasures and needs
I lack nothing
Except the power to walk through this screen

And enter the realm of the nameless
Dying from injustice
From hunger, cold, illness
From that which we can change

If only I could break
This illusioned window of warmth
Look within my depths
And find inner strength

To free those beings,
Who as we wish to live happy
In love, health and safety,
From the shackles of poverty and inhumanity

Mindful Eyes

They seem
silent stories
hungry bellies
swollen bodies
tearful eyes

But look within them you will find
Undying will to survive;
Desires to soar to unseen heights
To see the blind world with new eyes

Ask them what they want in life
They'll say they want as you or I
To quench the thirst within the mind
Amidst the dark to see the light

Lotus of the Lake

As a sea of blackened disparate waves,
Yearns to embrace lands of untouched sand;
And roll gently upon its grainy face,
Ease the weight of polluted liquid strands,
Release to Earth the ache of wasteful woes.
So too, the ill-fated poor of the slums,
Hold hopes of reaching steady shores.
Weighed heavily by the filth of the world,
Travel, in vain, the endless night;
Crash unbound in unnatural stance
Longing to escape the barren hands of plight,
To quiet roars of screaming starvation.
    In such anguish the impoverished go,
        Swallowed by the waves of their deathly foe.

On Poverty

Those souls who live without sweet luxuries
Realise a Truth more profound than time
Never will they be fools of humanity
Their lives tell tales in our subconscious minds
We know they grow from soil arid and dry
Yet vibrant, as blood red roses, they rise
Cherishing each ray of sunlight to thrive
In every drop of water seeing the ocean wide
They are the poets of resilience
Writing timeless rhymes with limited lines
As the rich grow tall with strength, they grow wise within
Gleaming as pure pearls betwixt tarnished sea shells
    Indeed, the poor are richer than the wealthy
    Behold this, unfathomed reality

Roots of Woe

The roots of poverty do stretch
Deep into the Earth's tender flesh
A vast, entanglement unblessed
Spreading unrested as contaminating cells

Drinking the tears of human misery
Emerging from seeds of broken dreams
Growing to the beat of human screams
Draining the Earth of vital energy

Poverty clenches to human violence
While silencing the hunger-stricken
Those poor facing abuse and offence
Have no defence against its relentlessness

But to look within and find peace

Ode to Poverty

1

You have shown your false colors
 On Earth's every living shore
As an empire you have conquered
 Great Nation's you have torn
Colonies stand in your name
 Entire cities bear your flag
 Indeed your presence casts
Shadows on those you've tagged
 All the dwellings in your domain
Stand draped in your dark rags

2

Even the strongest Nations tremble
 In fear and uncertainty
When your name they remember
 Knowing well your game of subtlety
How you enter a place with a quiet grace
 Smiling at those you want on your shelves
 Showing them sweet tricks with your magic sticks
Realms where they delve and lose themselves
 You lure them with their own desires
Indulge them in every tasty treat they fancy

Lotus of the Lake

3

When they find their lives
 Engulfed in false pleasures
Pierced deep with bitter lies
 It is too late to find again life's true treasures
Seeing their reflections in pools of filth
 Disgusted by their menacing presence
 Shamefully bowing their heads in defeat
 For they sense the barren road on which they tread,
Realising your malicious mastermind
 Has erased their destiny, and wrote a new script

4

In all your ragged splendour
 You have stolen another victory
By feeding humanity's lustful hunger
 You have beguiled the souls of these
Impoverished souls who now plant seeds of misery
 Bearing fruit of illness, and pain untold
 Rooted in soil stained with maya
Entrenched within your wretched threshold
 The deathly five—anger, lust, attachment, ego, greed
Fuel the growth of poverty's lair

On Poverty

5

As Buddha wisely proclaimed
 All pain has a source
Rooted in human desire
 As such misery is found
Where desire is unmet
 We have created that which we seek to diminish
 We have invited poverty home as a welcomed guest
Our love for luxury has watered your roots
 Our indulgence has tilled your fields
To lead selfless lives will put your growth to rest

Money Talks

Money talks
Money chats
Money walks
Money plays
Money sees
Money smiles
Money needs
Money feels
Money loves
Money hugs
Money masks
Money lasts
Money wines
Money dines
Money sings
Money swings
Money saves
Money lives
Money gives
Money caresses
Money frees
Money runs
Money strides
Money soars
Money flies
Money cares
Money dares
Money lasts
Money laughs

At our Ways...

SECTION 5

THE NEED FOR CHANGE

The poverty stricken people in India, predominantly from the Dalit class, often stand as outsiders in their own homeland. During the current international economic crisis, **the poor are sinking** into the sea of uncertainty, fear and helplessness. The voices of the silent slum dwellers must be heard, not only in India but worldwide. Their thoughts, desires, dreams have been muted by the cruel hand of poverty. It is time for them to speak and for the world to listen.

From my travels, I have discovered that pain and injustice are the result of fear, over-consumption and misunderstanding. The result of which are poverty, waste, environmental degradation, and abuse. We fuel the fire which consumes us. Allowing this destructive cycle to continue. Now, it is time to stop the cycle, look within and grow. We are already very late. It is time to stop.

The Need for Change

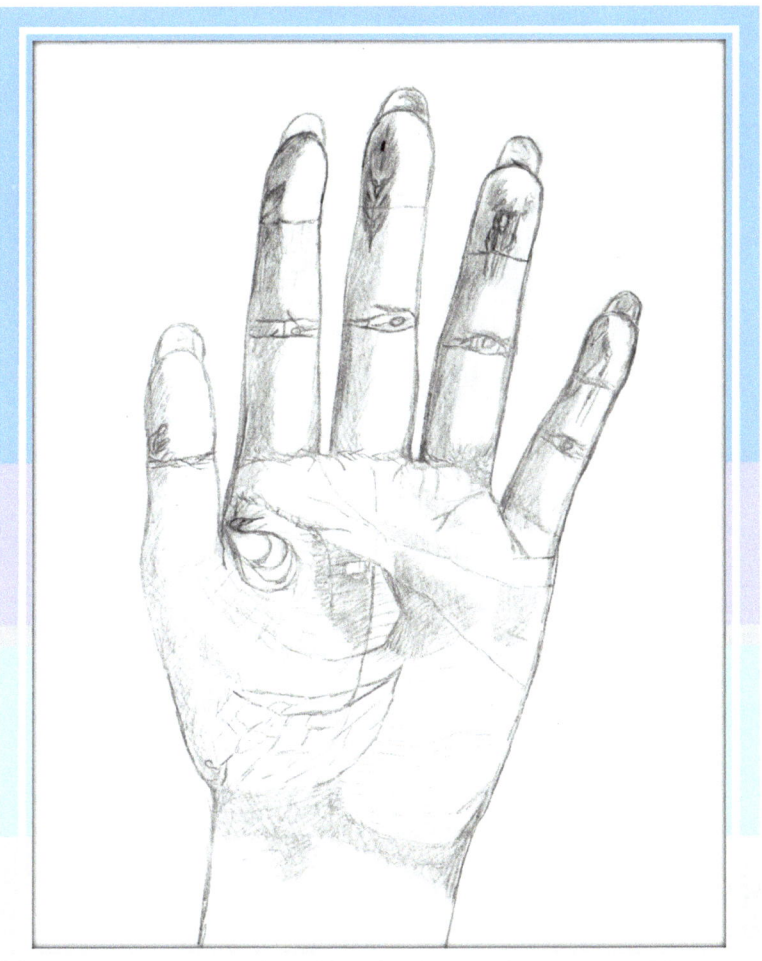

LOTUS OF THE LAKE

Stop
For a moment
Attempt to fathom
The fabric of
Our universe

Stop
A mere second
And think about
The essence of
Our livid Earth

Stop
For a time
And contemplate
Our place in the cosmos
Beside the Sun

Stop
And observe
The silent stars
Travelling from afar
Light years above

Stop
And behold
The flesh of
Our land unfold
Its intricate mould

Stop
Observe and feel
The ocean's gentle heart
Delve into its tender waves
And heal

The Need for Change

Stop
And close your eyes
Visualize
Our painted skies
Turn and unwind

Stop
And listen
To the whispering winds
Speaking to us
Every season

Stop
And sweep the skies
For airborne life
Diverse birds of flight
Watch them rise

Stop
And speak
To the fruitful trees
Springing tall from tiny seeds
It is us they seek

Stop
And smell
The bliss of flowers
Feel their tender power
Upon them dwell

Stop
Speak to those in need
Think of their lives
Help them climb
Fulfill their dreams

Lotus of the Lake

Stop
And follow
The path within you
Listen to the Truths
Unveil the layers of your soul

End

I have a suggestion
To end oppression
The corruption
Such suppression

Of Humans
Animals
Countries

Entrenched in fear
Clenched by hunger
Ditched by glamour
Drained by labour

Women
Migrants
Children

Wrapped in danger
Silenced by strangers
Trapped in torture
Whipped by anger

They need reconciliation
Knowledge
Liberation

To achieve an education
Integration with the nation
Freedom from destruction
Through government reparation

LOTUS OF THE LAKE

Build fewer malls
Parking stalls
Gaming halls

Build proper homes for the poor to own
Build schools specialized for tortured youth
Build programs to reconstruct addicts, the alone
Build communities from energy and hope

Allow the last
The least
The littlest to soar

Through the skies to fly unbound
Through the seas to hear nature's sounds
Through the gates of forest grounds
Through the doors to run homebound

Then we'll see
Unity
Peace
Harmony

Cloudy Steps

If I could bring the children here
To the peaks of tearless clouds
Lying in utter peace unfound
As endless icy arctic sheets

They would play
Upon the cloudy plain
With few cares about human pain
Rolling about on tufts of air

Building lofty castles
Surrounded by swaying streams
And laughing cherry trees
Among hills of utter majesty

They would watch with
The beauty of our sphere
Its sublime essence, its peace
And know Truth is always near

Each morning they would wake
Full of joy...never fear, or dismay

Changing Statistics

The shanty towns that choke the cities of Africa and Asia are experiencing unstoppable growth, expanding by more than a million people every week, according to the "state of the world's population" report.

When confronted with statistics on poverty, those who live above the poverty line, often claim, "It's so sad. We wish we could help but we don't know what to do."

How can we make the unwilling, realise the need? If we do not think of solutions for those on the lowest rungs of society, the entire fabric of our planet will be unstitched. We often think that those who suffer are the "others." The Truth is, we are them—the poor. They are us. We are one—all part of an immense, intricate web of life...all connected. If one part of the web falls, its entirety is affected.

In many countries around the world individuals above the poverty line appear to be "too busy" to worry about two of the fastest growing epidemics infecting the world—global poverty and global warming. In their comfortable worlds, individuals are well distracted by media, work, kids, family, friends and parties. Thus, they do not have the "time" to think about how to help. The problems of poverty and global warming seem distant as they are not sitting on their dinner plate or in their backyard.

Truth can be denied only a short while. If we do not **see** a problem, does it **cease** to exist? Although cancer patients cannot see cancer cells spreading, growing, multiplying within them, the infected cells continue to grow. Often, cancer patients realise they are infected when it is too late to heal. In the same way, poverty is growing as an infectious cancer throughout the world. It is silent, yet widespread and it has the ability to devastate humanity. If we are too busy to stop this infection, and if we cannot collectively think of a cure—we as a human society must rethink the essence of our existence.

The Need for Change

A world in which one succeeds and another fails is not a world—it is a purgatory of life. A world in which a few laugh, playing in the lap of luxury, while billions drown in the depths of disease and poverty, is unjust. A mere 2% of the world's population holds 90% of world's wealth clenched within its fists. As such, the majority of the world's children do not get to achieve their innate potential.

Earthly Robe

Though they come from anguished lands
Fruitless, rootless, soiled, stained
Filled with cries of woe, of pain
Wearing weathered, tattered rags

To me they are no different
Than those who live well nourished
In warm worlds of joyful bliss
Where youth unfolds as it is dreamt

Within each poor and each rich
Lies a deep well of Truth
Upon which lotuses bloom
Kissed by the sweet sun within

Outer flesh divides both ends,
Hiding unfound depths of life,
Concealing Truths of our minds
Enveloped words of silence

Fancy cars, and diamond rings
Ironed suits with cufflink shirts
Styled hair with subtle tints
Don't make us what we are within

Dollar bills, nor marble homes
Sparkling wines sipped with red lips
Skin tight jeans, branded Miss Sixty
Cannot plate our souls in gold

The priceless jewels which lie
Beyond reach of human eyes
Can neither be bought nor sold
They multiply over time
By the sound choices in our lives

SECTION 6

UNITED WE STAND

Solidarity

In the light of current global turmoil and injustice, humans need to unite in solidarity, contemplate and create global solutions. Every species on earth has the instinct to survive and reproduce. Yet, only humans have the ability to commit conscious acts of altruism. We have an invaluable gift of giving. As such, we are the only organisms on earth who can reverse the current plagues infecting our world through reconstruction. In many ways we have the responsibility to end ills such as poverty, inequality, injustice, suppression and global warming because we have caused them. The first step to global healing is realization—action follows. In a united and organized effort we can evaluate global issues and assist underclasses in becoming self-reliant and independent.

In order to assist the "bottom billion"[6] through sustained "self-reliance,"[7] widespread educational reform focused on the empowerment of children, is urgently needed. This can take the shape of international crisis intervention, strategic international development aid, NGO educational assistance programs, or new government policies prioritizing educational mandates. Through such reforms, individuals in even the most destitute regions of the world may have the opportunity to realise their innate potential and achieve higher standards of living.

On the Wings of Hope: Fly

The bright sunrise
Carries the skies
And every child

Upon rays they fly
Soaring high
Upon the lofty
Wings of Hope

Soar above,
Soar and thrive
Ride upon
The rays of time

Unity

I have envisioned
A world without divisions
Where all live in ease
The breeze, trees, seas, all beings

I have seen this world
Unfold before my yearning eyes
Emerging from one mould
Giving rise to all forms of life

In this world all are one
There is no distinction inside
Young or old, man or mouse
Between earth or sky, you or I

In this world there is Peace
Here abides true unity
Not only among humanity
But among every earthly entity

Here, animals do not fear
Being boxed in cages
By treacherous keepers
Wasting their worth in wretched rage

Here, humans love
Nature, and don't ravage its flesh
As if it were born
Only for their pleasure

They do not steal
Rather instil love and life into Earth
As blood given to the dying ill
They sustain it with care and breath

UNITED WE STAND

Species of the wild
Teach humans how to transcend
Maya and live in symbiosis
Together, in rhythmic silence

Humans do not lock
Themselves behind iron doors
Enclosed wooden homes
Afraid from the open air

They long to live
Immersed in the Earth
In the silent, harmless
Dirt which gives us birth

Human thought can surmise
That the bite of a bee
Or the pestering fly
Harm less than the sting of human misery

Thus, they do not shackle
Any part of the intricate universe.
Here all live untackled,
To enjoy freedom and strength

They realise, within all beings
Dwell the Earth, Wind, Fire, Water
As within the Earth
Dwell animals, humans, insects, trees, birds

In this world, the children sing
Verses of truth
When the Earth brings
Bountiful fruits

For all to enjoy

One Clay

The Arbutus Tree does proclaim
We are made but of one clay
Yielding beauty in every shape
Revealing new colours everyday

We emerge from a single sea
Of symmetry, beauty and peace
In every being behold these three
Not one is found without their grace

On Tolstoy

If
We seek to
Help those who
Stand beside us. The
Beings who we are with
At any given moment, we will
Achieve harmony within ourselves and with the
Universe. If we believe the most important time
Is now. The most important ones are the ones we
Are with, and the right thing to do is to
Help those we are with. We will not need to
Venture very far to discover the Truth. In fact it lies within
Us. It will help us find lasting inner peace, build castles in the
depths of our souls.

LOTUS OF THE LAKE

oppression	hatred	hunger
corruption	war	fear
greed	African crisis	drought
ignorance	malfeasance	image

Urgencies of our World

bad leadership	pollution	inequality
Abuse of power	poverty	Betrayal
Violence	Corporate Abuse	Genocide
Power	Greed	Exploitation
Refugees	Inhumanity	Envy

UNITED WE STAND

Respect	Equality	Compassion
God	harmony	Truth
Peace	No drugs	No weapons
Guru	Faith	Light
Human Rights	Universal Unity	Fair Trade

Global Solutions

Universal Harmony	Interdependence	Tolerance
Knowledge	**Understanding**	**Wisdom**
Governmental Policy	Buddhism	Generosity
Integrity	Political Infrastructure	Socialism
Global Governance	Freedom	Love

Ek Ong Kaar[8]
-Guru Nanak Dev Ji

Though we each have a unique experience on earth, we all walk on a single path towards inevitable death. Though many, varied in form, we are one. Our inner beings are intricately intermingled with everything that is—the vast web of life. What we do today affects every part of the living world in some capacity. It is important to consider the impacts our decisions will have not only on humans but on every living species on earth.

Art

We too, are part
Of this pristine
Landscape of earth

The mountain streams
Forested hills,
Valleys of green

As the stars
Nebulas of space
As all are

A piece of this universal canvas
Painted
And perfected

With every stroke
Every shade
Of life and love

We too are colours
In this work
Beautifying all that is

We too, are art

Awake

Awaken the heart to the sweet
Tune of personal liberty
Allow all inner realities
Swim, soar, sail earthly seas

We are...we are from one sea
Of ultimate harmony and peace
With inner Truth released
One is merged with the entirety

Seed

See yourself
In every living seed
Upon this plain of green
Know we are all the same

The mould of nature
And its creatures
Was borne
From one clay mound

Carefully formed with love
In shapes diverse
All with unique beauty
All with creativity

The success of one
Is the victory of all
The fall of one
Is the loss of all

We are connected
From within
United we win
Some see this some don't

Now, those in need
Cry out for our help
If we each
Take one hand

We will free,
Not only them,
But ourselves
From bitter winds

Suraj[9]

Created by the warming sun
All beings share its grace
Of power, Truth and light
To give, to live, and to create

Not one of us is without the sun
Within our core it lies
Warming our heavy hearts
Through the seasons of our lives

Every eye beholds the light
Of that single luminous star
Somehow it burns with splendour
Brighter with every earthly hour

Even through these cloudy days
It shines unfurling its crimson face
The grey skies of human plight
Do not taint its endless living rays

And when dark days overshadow
The joy in our searching eyes
We should seek the light deep within
Instilled in us by the sun of skies

If looking within you find not
Hope for life or healing dreams
Then look up at the living sky
And seek that which instils life in thee

Two Paths prevail in life

One towards
One against
The Light

Face of Gold

I journey the wild world and behold
Towering forests evergreen
Bordered by fresh rivers of gold
Under the glowing sun pristine
Veiled at eve with moonlit haze
Where only stars and salmon shine

Beyond this green I discover
Scented floral paths of red earth
Adorned by sweet coconut groves
Of palm trees bearing fruit of milk
Spilling into hills and valleys of carved stone
Chiselled as sculptures of the seasons

I travel further still, following the hawk
To lands of treasured greenery
Upon the coast, castles of flawless rock
Where the air is thick with heat
And the land abundant with fruit
Ripened with all shades of the spectrum

Though bearing different complexions
All features of earth, bathed by the silver moon
And warmed by the golden sun, are one
Venturing east, west, south and north
I view one earthly visage
Immaculate with beauty and worth

Light, earth, water, and air,
Upon the adorned face of earth,
Are moulded from a single substance
So too, in the eyes of worldly beings
I see one purpose, one ache
To live in love, in joy, in peace

SECTION 7

KNOWLEDGE, WISDOM, AND UNDERSTANDING

Out in the open wisdom calls aloud,
She raises her voice in the public square.
-PROVERBS 1:20 (TNIV)

With effective and sustainable humanitarian aid and through the empowerment of local children and adults, positive social change is possible. Even as a twelve year old child visiting the Punjab with my family, I knew that for me and my family, education was the way forward and the way for us to achieve our dreams. Today, I look at the world and say—education is the way forward and the way to achieve world without divisions...without poverty.

Education and Human Security

In terms of personal security, educational training gives children the opportunity to make their own informed decisions, lessening their chances of being exploited. "Schools are not just institutions for imparting information. They are a place where children can acquire social skills and self-confidence, where they learn about their countries, their cultures and the world they live in" (UNESCO, 2009, p. 24). Through an education, talented and gifted children such as, Rajesh, Maruthi, Muskaan and Raju, who would have otherwise "blushed unseen," can enjoy opportunities to attain higher standards of living. In this way, they can realize their full potential through various educational avenues and "share their sweetness" with the world.

It is noted in the UNESCO report: *Education for All*, that "no country has ever reduced poverty over the medium term without sustained economic growth. Education plays a critical role in producing the learning and skills needed to generate the productivity gains that fuel growth" (UNESCO, 2009, p. 30). As noted above, an enhanced education system may allow individuals to invest in the social and economic aspects of society, enhancing their human security and quality of life through personal knowledge and skills. This can lead to a more meritocratic society where people have the ability to realise their potential through work ethic and perseverance. This way, gives people the tools to succeed on the basis of personal merit rather than familial networking, socio-economic status, or corrupt practices. Education may also help reduce the divide between the elite and individuals from lower socio-economic areas.

It is important to specify that the *public* education system in a state must be strengthened in order to reduce widespread poverty, and to bring equal opportunity and balance to a society. If private sector education grows at a faster pace, receiving more funding and resources, it may block access for children from underprivileged backgrounds to compete for employment, widening economic disparities. This is currently occurring in states such as, India, Latin America, the Caribbean and various countries in Sub-Saharan Africa. Here, affluent individuals are sending their children to private or international institutions while the public education system for poorer children is severely underfunded and sometimes non-existent. In some cases, children are banned from attending public schools based on their social class.

Without the opportunity to acquire marketable skills and knowledge, the majority of impoverished children will end up pan handling or in menial labour jobs. It must be acknowledged that "no country can afford the inefficiencies that arise when people are denied opportunities for education because they are poor, female or members of a particular social group" (UNESCO, 2009, p. 27). To deny individuals a basic education is to deny them an integral part of being human. Learning and advanced knowledge retention capacities differentiate humans from every other living organism on earth. All humans should have the choice and the opportunity to cultivate their minds.

Enough for All

In our home upon the earth
So many starve
This earth, so abundant
There is enough food for all

We can feed the world thrice over, with leftovers
Every child
This is no lie
There is enough food for all

The earth gives her fruit
Free
No fees
There is enough food for all

This world allows all souls
To walk on its every path
Earth, a borrowed land
We must leave enough food for all

Let us open our doors
Break through the walls
Answer every child's call
For, there is enough food for all

Celestial Sky

Watch the smiling morning sky.
The sun glances at the playful wind
Telling tales of ancient Earth
And of their unshaken bond.

Their union lasting through
The ages of nature's growth,
And the plague of human woe.
Their bond will prevail until Earth's unsown.

Neither time nor trial will taint their fate
The sun and wind work in rhythm
Dancing on the age-less face
Of this blue sky of hope

So consumed by their own affair
Harmonious in all they do
Creating the spectrum of colour
Giving life to inspire Truth

The clouds sit on the steps of their stage
As the sun and wind waltz through time
The winds blow through the sun's warming rays
Receiving streaks of light on their breath

The winds bring clouds as soft as snow
To reveal the beauty of morning light
Allowing human eyes to find
The perfect shape of the sun sublime

Through these delicate windows,
Behold spherical light
As it rises high in our globe
Preparing to warm our earthly sky

Knowledge, Wisdom, and Understanding

The love within this saffron sphere
Extends through time to reach the wind
Its limbs, the rays, shoot through our lair
To feel the gentle gestures of the breeze

Observe this laughing sky
Perhaps you as I will find
Peace in plunder and plight
Hope on wings of time

*"Be the change you want
to see in the world."*
-Mahatma Gandhi

While trekking the East for answers to my long list of questions, I journeyed even further within myself realising that throughout my existence, the Truth has lied **within. I needed only to stop and listen to the intuitive voice inside which so simply states—change begins with you.**

Hungry Planet

So few of us
Own all too much
Still desires
Plague our minds

A mere handful of us
Have enough to eat
Yet still we feel
Empty bellies

We fail to see
Those who truly
Starve day after day
And accept their lives this way

Why should they grow thin?
And we seek to win
More fruit than we need
Fruit with which we can feed

The World

The Global Web

The global economic system and urban expansion have interwoven convenience, efficiency, rapid information management and communication into the fabric of modern living in many parts of the world. However, in the same global tapestry we have also seen heightened poverty, child labour, human trafficking, and erosion of working conditions for women, disadvantaged individuals, and migrant workers. In order to catalyze long term improvement in the global state of child labour and the working conditions of other disadvantaged individuals, broad-based public education, state reform at the legislative levels, and equal opportunity for all people is imperative. With the issue of child poverty, as with a number of societal problems, strategies and policies must be developed at the community level, national level and at the international community level. The technological advancement and global interconnectedness of today can be utilized to mitigate current trends in poverty, inequality and worker exploitation through goal-directed, collective and synchronised action plans extending from the community to the entire global web of life.

Part of the proceeds from book sales will go towards the further development of various Children's Homes found throughout India including Bangalore, Punjab, Mumbai, Pune, Assam and Benares. The improvements will include, sanitation and maintenance; the employment of full-time house mothers to care for the younger children; initiation of garden and mural projects; management and reconstruction of sleeping and bathing facilities; the introduction of nutritious meals; the purchase of clean uniforms and private lockers for the children; and the introduction of a Sponsorship Program to promote Post Secondary Education among the children.

Endnotes

[1] Gray, Thomas. "Elegy Written in a Country Church-Yard" (1751).

[2] Business Today. Ifzal Ali, Chief Economist, ADB, Bloomberg. October 30, 2007. http://businesstoday.intoday.in/index.

[3] Gray, Thomas. "Elegy Written in a Country Church-Yard" (1751). "Mute Inglorious Milton" here references the seventeenth century English poet John Milton, author of *Paradise Lost*.

[4] Muskaan: Literal translation from Hindi is "smile."

[5] Millennium Development Goals Indicators (2008). The official United Nations site for MDG indicators.

[6] Collier, Paul. *The Bottom Billion: Why the Poorest Countries are Failing and What Can Be Done About It* (2007). New York: Oxford University Press Inc.

[7] Helin, Calvin. *Dances with Dependency: Out of Poverty through Self-Reliance* (2008). Woodland Hills, California: Ravencrest Publishing.

[8] Ek Ong Kaar: The first words of Guru Nanak Dev Ji following his enlightenment in the Kala Dhariya (Black River) in Punjab. This was later written in the Japuji Sahib prayer, which is the first prayer found in the Holy Book, the Sri Guru Granth Sahib Ji. Ek Ong Kaar refers to the oneness of the spiritual and the physical realms, that the metaphysical (ong) is intermingled with the physical (kaar). They are essentially one (ek)

[9] Suraj: Literal translation from Hindi is "sun."